Pocket Edition

100 FACTS

ANCIENT EGYPT

Jane Walker

Consultant: Rupert Matthews

Miles Kelly

First published in 2001 by Miles Kelly Publishing Ltd
Harding's Barn, Bardfield End Green, Thaxted, Essex, CM6 3PX, UK
Copyright © Miles Kelly Publishing Ltd 2001

This edition updated 2014, printed 2020

2 4 6 8 10 9 7 5 3

Publishing Director Belinda Gallagher
Creative Director Jo Cowan
Editorial Director Rosie Neave
Designers Rob Hale, Andrea Slane
Cover Designer Simon Lee
Image Manager Liberty Newton
Production Elizabeth Collins, Jennifer Brunwin-Jones
Reprographics Stephan Davis
Indexer Jane Parker
Assets Lorraine King

ISBN 978-1-78617-610-3

Printed in China

British Library Cataloguing-in-Publication Data
A catalogue record for this book is available from the British Library

ACKNOWLEDGEMENTS

The publishers would like to thank the following sources for theuse of their photographs:
Key: t = top, b = bottom, l = left, r = right, c = centre, bg = background

Alamy 28 Miguel Cuenca **Fotolia.com** 9 Konstantin Sutyagin **Getty** 23 The Print Collector
Glow Images 40(b) SuperStock; 45(b) Werner Forman Archive
National Geographic Creative 30–31(b), 36–37, 41, 44–45 H.M. Herget
Shutterstock.com 2–3 Nagib; 9 ChameleonsEye; 10(bg) diversepixel; 10–11(b) leoks; 14–15(bg) diversepixel;
16–17(bg) mountainpix; 34–35(bg) Luisa Fumi; 42(b) Architecteur; 43(b) Vladimir Korostyshevskiy;
42–43(bg) Eugene Sergeev; 46–47 WitR **Science Photo Library** 18–19 Henning Dalhoff
Topfoto 25(t) The Granger Collection; 26(t) The Granger Collection; 43(t) 2005

All other photographs are from:
Corel, digitalSTOCK, digitalvision, John Foxx, PhotoAlto,
PhotoDisc, PhotoEssentials, PhotoPro, Stockbyte

Every effort has been made to acknowledge the source and copyright holder of each picture.
Miles Kelly Publishing apologises for any unintentional errors or omissions.

Made with paper from a sustainable forest

www.mileskelly.net

Pocket Edition 100 FACTS

ANCIENT EGYPT

Contents

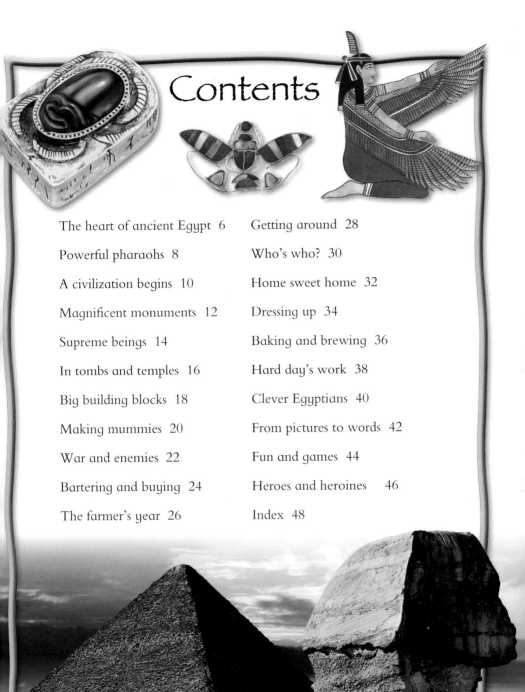

The heart of ancient Egypt

1 **Without the river Nile, the civilization of ancient Egypt might never have existed.** The Nile provided water for drinking and watering crops. Every year its floods left a strip of rich, dark soil on both sides of the river where farmers grew crops. The Egyptians called their country *Kemet*, which means 'black land', after this dark soil. The Nile was also a trade route.

▼ The Nile supported many activities such as trade and farming. It was also an important transportation route, with people and goods travelling by boat.

Powerful pharaohs

2 The rulers of ancient Egypt were called pharaohs. The word 'pharaoh' means great house. The pharaoh was the most important and powerful person in the country. Many people believed he was a god.

▼ These people are paying tribute to the pharaoh. They have come from nearby countries to pay him respect and offer him gifts.

The pharaoh is holding the symbols of his rule – the hook (right) and flail (left)

◀ On her wedding day, the bride wore a long linen dress or tunic.

3 The pharaoh often married a close female relative, such as his sister or half-sister. In this way the blood of the royal family remained pure. The title of 'pharaoh' was usually passed on to the eldest son of the pharaoh's most important wife.

▲ At Abu Simbel Rameses II built four statues of himself, each over 20 metres tall.

4 Rameses II ruled for more than 60 years. He was the only pharaoh to carry the title 'the Great' after his name. Rameses was a great builder and brave soldier. He was also the father of a large number of children – 96 boys and 60 girls.

9

A civilization begins

5 More than 7000 years ago, people from Syria and the Sahara moved into Egypt. They learned how to farm crops, and settled in villages along the banks of the Nile and the Nile Delta. By about 5500 years ago, there were two kingdoms, Upper Egypt and Lower Egypt.

6 The history of ancient Egypt began more than 5000 years ago. The first period was called the Old Kingdom, when the Egyptians built the Great Pyramids. Next came the Middle Kingdom and finally the New Kingdom.

MEDITERRANEAN SEA
Nile Delta
Alexandria
Giza
Saqqara· Memphis
El-Amarna
LOWER EGYPT Valley of the Kings· ·Karnak
Thebes· ·Luxor
·Aswan
·Abu Simbel
RED SEA
UPPER EGYPT
River Nile
NUBIAN DESERT

▲ Egypt was split into Lower Egypt (Nile Delta) and Upper Egypt (Nile Valley). Desert conditions meant that people settled along the banks of the Nile.

▼ Historians have divided Egyptian history into a number of periods depending on who was ruling Egypt at the time.

King Narmer, also called Menes, unites Egypt and records his deeds on the Narmer palette

Egypt's first pyramid, the Step Pyramid, was built in 2650 BC

People introduced gods for all different areas of life

The Hyksos people invaded in 1670 BC and introduced the chariot

Nilometers kept track of the height of the river, which was important for crops

| 3100–2750 BC EARLY DYNASTIC PERIOD (Dynasties I and II) | 2750–2250 BC OLD KINGDOM (Dynasties III–VI) | 2250–2025 BC FIRST INTERMEDIATE PERIOD (Dynasties VII–X) | 2025–1627 BC MIDDLE KINGDOM (Dynasties XI–XIII) | 1648–1539 BC SECOND INTERMEDIATE PERIOD (Dynasties XIV–XVII) |

▶ A vizier checks grain brought in from the harvest while a criminal awaits punishment. Viziers were among the most powerful people in ancient Egypt.

7 Officials called viziers helped the pharaoh to govern Egypt. Each ruler appointed two viziers – one each for Upper and Lower Egypt. Each vizier was in charge of a number of royal overseers. Each overseer was responsible for a particular area of government, for example the army or granaries where the grain was stored.

8 Over 30 different dynasties ruled ancient Egypt. A dynasty is a line of rulers from the same family.

I DON'T BELIEVE IT!

Farmers tried to bribe tax collectors by offering them goats or ducks in exchange for a smaller tax charge.

The tomb of pharaoh Tutankhamun was discovered in 1922

The god Ra became Amun-Ra, the king of the gods

In 332 BC Alexander the Great conquered Egypt and founded the city of Alexandria

Queen Cleopatra was the last ruler of the Ptolemaic Period

The Roman Emperor Octavian conquered Egypt in 30 BC

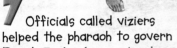

**1539–1070 BC
NEW KINGDOM**
(Dynasties XVIII–XX)

**1070–653 BC
THIRD
INTERMEDIATE PERIOD**
(Dynasties XXI–XXV)

**664–332 BC
LATE PERIOD**
(Dynasties XXVI–XXXI)

**332–30 BC
PTOLEMAIC PERIOD**

**30 BC–AD 395
ROMAN PERIOD**

Magnificent monuments

9 **The pyramids at Giza are more than 4500 years old.** They were built for three kings, Khufu, Khafre and Menkaure. The biggest, the Great Pyramid, took more than 20 years to build. Thousands of workers were needed to complete the job.

Pyramid of Menkaure

Pyramid of Khafre

► The Great Pyramid is built from over two million blocks of limestone. It stands about 140 metres high.

Mastabas

Great Pyramid of Khufu

King's chamber

Queen's chamber

Underground chamber

Mortuary temple

Queens' pyramids

QUIZ

1. For which king was the Great Pyramid built?

2. In the Great Pyramid, which corridor lead to the king's chamber?

3. Where was the first step pyramid built?

Answers:
1. King Khufu 2. The Grand Gallery 3. Saqqara

10 **The Great Pyramid, the biggest of the three pyramids, was built as a burial place for King Khufu.** He ordered three smaller pyramids to be built beside it – for his three main wives. The boat that probably carried Khufu's body to his tomb was buried in a pit alongside the pyramid.

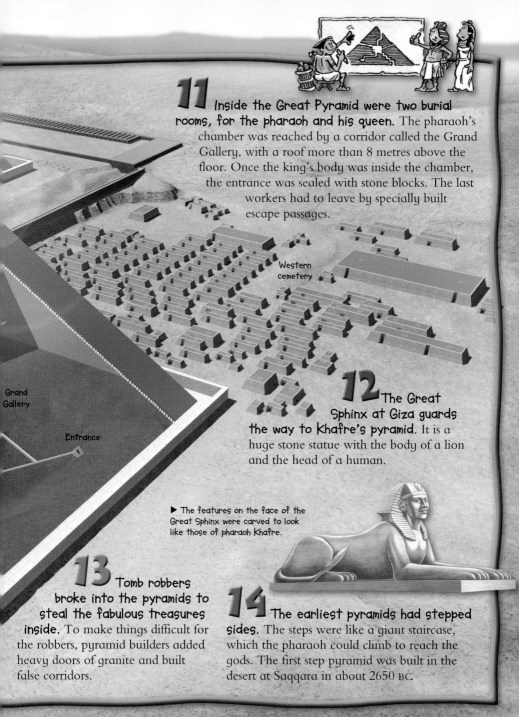

11 Inside the Great Pyramid were two burial rooms, for the pharaoh and his queen. The pharaoh's chamber was reached by a corridor called the Grand Gallery, with a roof more than 8 metres above the floor. Once the king's body was inside the chamber, the entrance was sealed with stone blocks. The last workers had to leave by specially built escape passages.

Western cemetery

Grand Gallery

Entrance

12 The Great Sphinx at Giza guards the way to Khafre's pyramid. It is a huge stone statue with the body of a lion and the head of a human.

▶ The features on the face of the Great Sphinx were carved to look like those of pharaoh Khafre.

13 Tomb robbers broke into the pyramids to steal the fabulous treasures inside. To make things difficult for the robbers, pyramid builders added heavy doors of granite and built false corridors.

14 The earliest pyramids had stepped sides. The steps were like a giant staircase, which the pharaoh could climb to reach the gods. The first step pyramid was built in the desert at Saqqara in about 2650 BC.

Supreme beings

15 **The ancient Egyptians worshipped many gods and goddesses.** The most important was Ra, the sun god. People believed that he was swallowed up each evening by the sky goddess Nut. During the night Ra travelled the underworld and was reborn each morning.

16 **A god was often shown as an animal, or as half-human, half-animal.** Bastet was goddess of cats, musicians and dancers. Cats were sacred in ancient Egypt. When a pet cat died, it was wrapped and laid in a cat-shaped coffin before burial in a cat cemetery. The moon god Thoth usually had the head of an ibis, but he was sometimes shown as a baboon. People believed that hieroglyphic writing came from Thoth.

Amun-Ra
Sun god

▶ Crocodiles were kept at the temples of the god Sobek.

Nut
Sky goddess

Sobek
God of the Nile

Bastet
Goddess of cats and music

◀ The sun god Ra was popular in Lower Egypt. The people of Upper Egypt linked him to their own god Amun, so both gods became known as Amun-Ra.

17 As god of the dead, Osiris was in charge of the underworld. Ancient Egyptians believed that dead people travelled to the kingdom of the underworld below the Earth. Osiris and his wife Isis were the parents of the god Horus, protector of the pharaoh.

18 Anubis was in charge of preparing bodies to be mummified. This work was known as embalming. Because jackals were often found near cemeteries, Anubis, who watched over the dead, was given the form of a jackal. Egyptian priests often wore Anubis masks.

19 Pharaoh Amenhotep IV worshipped one god – Aten the creator. He closed down temples to all other gods and even changed his name to Akhenaten, which means 'Spirit of Aten'.

Osiris
God of the dead

Horus
God of the sky

Thoth
Moon god

Isis
Goddess of rebirth

Anubis
God of the underworld

15

In tombs and temples

20 From about 2150 BC pharaohs were not buried in pyramids, but in tombs in the Valley of the Kings. This remote place was surrounded by steep cliffs on the west bank of the Nile opposite the city of Thebes. Some tombs were cut into the sides of the cliffs, others were built deep underground.

21 The riches in the tombs attracted robbers. The entrance to the Valley of the Kings was guarded, but robbers broke into every tomb except one within 1000 years. The only one they missed was the boy king Tutankhamun's, and even this had been partially robbed and re-sealed.

▼ Tutankhamun's sarcophagus was inside a set of four wooden shrines big enough to contain a modern car.

Wrapped mummy

Inner gold coffin

Middle wooden coffin

Outer wooden coffin

Inner coffin cover

Middle coffin cover

Outer coffin cover

Sarcophagus

22 Archaeologist Howard Carter discovered the tomb of Tutankhamun in 1922. An archaeologist is someone who studies ancient sites and objects. The body of Tutankhamun was found inside a nest of three mummy cases, encased within a sarcophagus (stone coffin).

24 Building work at the Temples of Karnak lasted 1700 years from about 1900 BC. There were three great temples dedicated to the gods Amun-Re, Mut and Montu plus dozens of smaller temples and chapels. Today, millions of people flock to the area to see the remains of the once splendid temple structures.

▼ The courtyard in the Temple of Amun-Re at Karnak was entered through a massive gateway, or pylon, about 17 metres tall.

23 The Egyptians built fabulous temples to worship their gods. Powerful priests ruled over the temples, and the riches and lands attached to them. Many of the finest temples were dedicated to Amun-Ra, king of the gods.

Big building blocks

25 Each block used to build the Great Pyramid weighed as much as two and a half adult elephants! Labourers used copper chisels and saws to cut and shape the stones before dragging them on wooden sledges to the base of the pyramid.

▶ Pyramids were built using large blocks of stone dragged into position by teams of workmen.

The finished pyramids had a bright, white casing of polished limestone to reflect the rays of the Sun, and the top may have been covered by gold leaf

The huge stones had to be levered into exactly the right position

Wooden sledge for dragging stone blocks

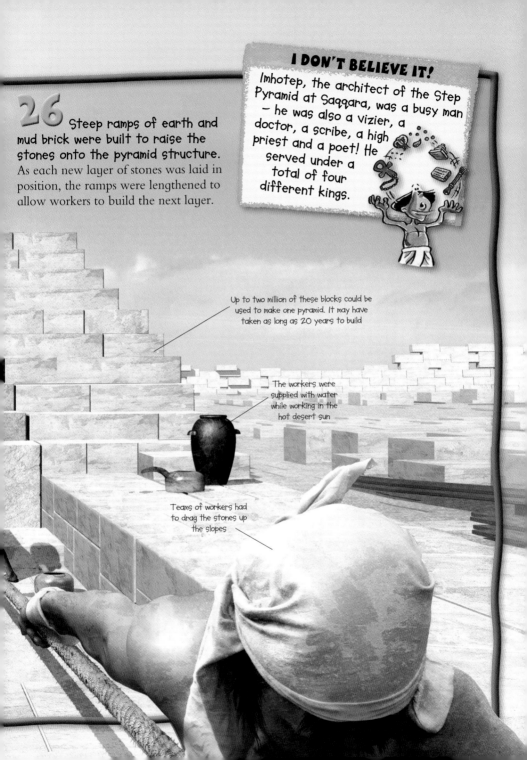

26 Steep ramps of earth and mud brick were built to raise the stones onto the pyramid structure. As each new layer of stones was laid in position, the ramps were lengthened to allow workers to build the next layer.

I DON'T BELIEVE IT!

Imhotep, the architect of the Step Pyramid at Saqqara, was a busy man — he was also a vizier, a doctor, a scribe, a high priest and a poet! He served under a total of four different kings.

Up to two million of these blocks could be used to make one pyramid. It may have taken as long as 20 years to build

The workers were supplied with water while working in the hot desert sun

Teams of workers had to drag the stones up the slopes

Making mummies

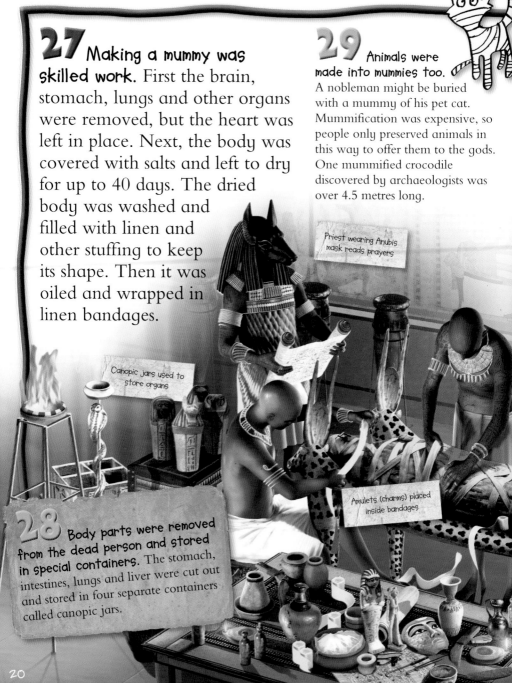

27 **Making a mummy was skilled work.** First the brain, stomach, lungs and other organs were removed, but the heart was left in place. Next, the body was covered with salts and left to dry for up to 40 days. The dried body was washed and filled with linen and other stuffing to keep its shape. Then it was oiled and wrapped in linen bandages.

29 **Animals were made into mummies too.** A nobleman might be buried with a mummy of his pet cat. Mummification was expensive, so people only preserved animals in this way to offer them to the gods. One mummified crocodile discovered by archaeologists was over 4.5 metres long.

Priest wearing Anubis mask reads prayers

Canopic jars used to store organs

Amulets (charms) placed inside bandages

28 **Body parts were removed from the dead person and stored in special containers.** The stomach, intestines, lungs and liver were cut out and stored in four separate containers called canopic jars.

30 A mask was fitted over the face of a mummy. The ancient Egyptians believed that the mask would help the dead person's spirit to recognize the mummy later on. A pharaoh's mummy mask was made of gold and precious stones.

31 When ready for burial, a mummy was placed inside a special case. Some cases were simple wooden boxes, but others were shaped like mummies and richly decorated. The mummy case of an important person, such as a pharaoh or a nobleman, was sealed inside a stone coffin called a sarcophagus.

▼ The process of making mummies took place in sacred workshops and was accompanied by rituals and prayers.

It took many years of training to become a mummy-maker

Hundreds of metres of bandages were used

War and enemies

32 **Foot soldiers carried metal swords and spears, with shields made of wood or ox hide.** Later, soldiers were protected by body armour made from strips of leather.

▼ A pharaoh, wearing the blue war crown, rides into battle on a chariot.

▶ During the New Kingdom, Egypt formed a professional army of trained soldiers. They had strong shields and long, deadly spears.

33 **Soldiers fired arrows while riding in horse-drawn chariots.** Each chariot carried two soldiers and was pulled by a pair of horses. During the time of the New Kingdom (around 3500 years ago), this new kind of war weapon helped the Egyptians to defeat several invading armies.

34 **The Hyksos people conquered Egypt in about 1700 BC.** They ruled the Egyptians for 200 years. They introduced the horse, the chariot and other new weapons that the Egyptians eventually used to conquer an empire.

35 A Macedonian general called Ptolemy won control of Egypt in 323 BC. He was the first of several rulers who made up the Ptolemaic dynasty. Under the Ptolemies, the city of Alexandria, on the Mediterranean Sea, became the new Egyptian capital and an important city for art and culture.

36 The Sea People attacked Egypt during the reign of Rameses III. These raiders came from the northeastern corner of the Mediterranean. Rameses sent a fleet of ships to defeat them.

◄ The great harbours at Alexandria were guarded by the huge Pharos, the first lighthouse in the world and one of the Seven Wonders of the Ancient World.

23

Bartering and buying

37 **Before 500 BC, Egyptian traders did not use money to buy and sell goods.** Instead they bartered (exchanged goods) with other traders. Merchants visited lands bordering the Mediterranean Sea as well as lands to the south. They offered goods such as gold, a paper called papyrus, and cattle.

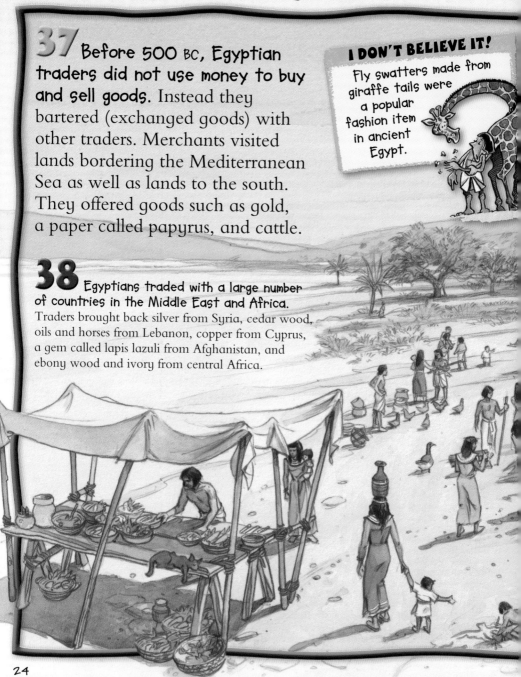

I DON'T BELIEVE IT!

Fly swatters made from giraffe tails were a popular fashion item in ancient Egypt.

38 **Egyptians traded with a large number of countries in the Middle East and Africa.** Traders brought back silver from Syria, cedar wood, oils and horses from Lebanon, copper from Cyprus, a gem called lapis lazuli from Afghanistan, and ebony wood and ivory from central Africa.

39 Merchants brought back exotic goods from the land of Nubia, to the south of Egypt. These included leopard skins, elephant tusks, ostrich feathers – and slaves. One of the main trading posts where goods were exchanged was the town of Kerma, on the river Nile beyond Egypt.

▶ A painting shows men from Nubia bringing goods to Egypt.

40 When goods were sold they were weighed using a balance and special copper weights called deben. An item could be exchanged for its equivalent weight in copper. A bed, for example, had a value of 25 deben. Pieces of gold and silver were also weighed and used as payment.

▲ A busy Egyptian trading market with people bartering for goods.

The farmer's year

41 **The farming year was divided into three seasons: the flood, the growing period and the harvest.** Most people worked on the land, but farmers could not work between July and November because the land was flooded. Instead, they helped to build the pyramids and royal palaces.

42 **The river Nile used to flood its banks in July each year.** The flood waters left a strip of rich, black soil, about 10 kilometres wide, along each bank. Apart from these fertile strips and a few scattered oases (pools of water in the desert) the rest of the land was mainly just sand.

▲ Water is lifted onto a field using a shaduf, just as is done in Egypt today.

44 **Water was lifted from the Nile using a shaduf.** It was a long pole with a wooden bucket hanging from a rope at one end, and a weight at the other. The pole was supported by a wooden frame. One person working alone could operate a shaduf.

◄ Tax collectors would often decide how rich a person was by counting how many cattle he owned.

43 **Egyptian farmers had to water their crops because of the hot, dry climate with no rain.** They dug special channels around their fields along which the waters of the Nile could flow. In this way farmers could water their crops all year round. This was called irrigation.

▲ Almost no rain fell on the dry, dusty farmland of ancient Egypt. No crops could grow properly without the water from the Nile.

45 Wooden ploughs pulled by oxen prepared the soil for planting. Seeds were mainly planted by hand. At harvest time, wooden sickles edged with stone teeth were used to cut the crops.

▲ A man ploughs a field of wheat or barley, assisted by his wife.

46 Harvesting grain was only the start of the process. In the threshing room people would beat the grain to separate it from the chaff, the shell, of the grain. It was then winnowed. Men would throw the grain and chaff into the air and fan away the chaff. The heavier grain dropped straight to the floor. The grain was then gathered up and taken to the granary to be stored.

47 Wheat and barley (for bread and beer) were the two main crops grown by the ancient Egyptians. They also grew grapes (for wine) and flax (to make linen). A huge variety of fruits and vegetables grew in the fertile soil, including dates, figs, cucumbers, melons, onions, peas, leeks and lettuces.

I DON'T BELIEVE IT!

Instead of using scarecrows, Egyptian farmers hired young boys to scare away the birds – they had to have a loud voice and a good aim with a slingshot!

▼ Winnowers separate the grain from the chaff.

48 Egyptian farmers kept cattle as well as goats, sheep, ducks and geese. Some farmers kept bees to produce honey, which was used for sweetening cakes and other foods.

Getting around

49 **The main method of transporting goods in ancient Egypt was by boat along the Nile.** The Nile is the world's longest river. It flows across the entire length of the desert lands of Egypt.

50 **The earliest kinds of boat were made from papyrus reeds.** They were propelled by a long pole and, later on, by oars. Gradually, wooden boats replaced the reed ones, and sails were added.

▲ Early boats were made from bundles of reeds tied together.

51 **A magnificent carved boat was built to carry the body of King Khufu at his funeral.** More than 43 metres long, it was built from planks of cedar wood. The boat was buried in a special pit next to the Great Pyramid.

▲ The Nile results from the joining of three great rivers — the White Nile, the Blue Nile and the Atbara.

52 **Transporting cattle across the Nile could be difficult.** Wide-bodied cargo boats were used to ferry cattle across the Nile. The animals stood on the deck during the crossing.

◀ In 1954, King Khufu's funerary boat was found buried at the foot of the Great Pyramid.

53 Wooden barges carried blocks of limestone across the river Nile for the pyramids and temples. The stone came from quarries on the opposite bank to the site of the pyramids. The granite used to build the insides of the pyramids came from much farther away – from quarries at Aswan 800 kilometres upstream.

▼ A merchant river boat powered by sails or oars.

▲ Blocks of stone are loaded on a boat to be taken along the Nile to a building site.

Who's who?

54 **People were divided into classes.** Farmers and tradesmen worked in businesses owned by the state or temples, and could not move class. Scribes and merchants could move, but were barely richer than farmers and tradesmen. Nobles and priests organized Egypt under the pharaoh's rule.

◀ The arrangement of Egyptian society can be shown as a pyramid shape. The pharaoh sits at the top, with unskilled labourers at the bottom.

Viziers and priests

Scribes and noblemen

Craftworkers and dancers

Peasant workers

55 **The man was the head of the household.** On his father's death, the eldest son inherited the family's land and riches. Women had rights and privileges too. They could own property and carry out business deals, and women from wealthy families could become doctors or priestesses.

I DON'T BELIEVE IT!

Wealthy Egyptians wanted servants in the afterlife too. They were buried with models of servants, called shabtis, that were meant to come to life and look after their dead owner!

▶ Family life played an important role in ancient Egypt. Couples could adopt children if they were unable to have their own.

56 Most ancient Egyptians lived along the banks of the river Nile or in the river valley. As Egypt became more powerful they spread out, up along the river Nile and around the Mediterranean Sea. Others lived by oases, pools of water in the desert.

57 Rich families had several servants, who worked as maids, cooks and gardeners. In large houses the servants had their own quarters separate from those of the family.

58 Dogs and cats were the main pets. Egyptians also kept pet monkeys and sometimes flocks of tame doves. Some people trained their pet baboons to climb fig trees and pick the ripe fruits.

59 Young children played with wooden and clay toys. Popular toys were carved animals – often with moving parts – spinning tops, toy horses, dolls and clay balls. Children also played games that are still played today, such as leapfrog and tug-o'-war.

Home sweet home

60 Houses were made from mud bricks dried in the sun. Straw and pebbles were added to the mud to make it strong. Tree trunks supported the flat roofs. Inside walls were plastered and often painted. The rich lived in big houses with several storeys. The poor often lived in a single room.

61 Rich families lived in spacious villas in the countryside. A typical villa had a pond filled with fish, a walled garden and an orchard of fruit trees.

62 Homes were furnished with wooden chairs, tables, chests and carved beds. A three- or four-legged footstool was a common item of furniture. Reed mats covered the floors.

Pots and plates were made of clay and fired in a hot kiln.

Bricks were made of mud and clay strengthened with straw and pebbles. They were packed in wooden frames and left to harden in the sun.

63 Food was cooked in a clay oven or over an open fire. Most kitchens had a cylinder-shaped oven made from bricks of baked clay. Wood or charcoal was burnt as fuel, and food was placed in two-handled pottery saucepans to cook.

64 Pottery lamps provided lighting. The container was filled with oil and a wick made of cotton or flax was burned. Houses had very small windows, and sometimes none at all, so there was often little natural light. Small windows kept out the strong sunlight, helping to keep houses cool.

Bread was the staple food. It was baked in a hot oven. The poor ate coarse brown bread and the rich ate white.

Beer was stored in pottery jars. Spices and dates were added to improve the taste.

Clothes were made with linen woven on a loom, from the fibres of the flax plant.

65 In most Egyptian homes there was a small shrine. Here, members of the family worshipped their household god.

66 In Egypt it was good to eat with your fingers! In rich households, servants would even bring jugs of water between courses so that people could rinse their hands.

Dressing up

67 **Egyptians wore lucky charms called amulets.** The charms were meant to protect the wearer from evil spirits and to bring good luck. One of the most popular ones was the eye of the god Horus. Children wore amulets shaped like fish to protect them from drowning in the river Nile.

▲ Scarab amulets were worn for good fortune. They were carved from gems and semi-precious stones.

68 **Both men and women wore eye make-up.** A black eye make-up, called kohl, was made from ground-up raw metals mixed with oil. The Egyptians believed it had healing powers and could restore bad eyesight and fight infections. People also used rouge for the cheeks and lips, face powder, paint for fingernails and hair dyes.

◀ A wealthy woman applying eye make-up before putting on her wig.

69 **Most clothes were made from light-coloured linen.** Women wore long dresses, often with pleated cloaks. Noblewomen's dresses were made of the best cloth with beads sewn onto it. Noblemen wore either robes or kilt-like skirts, a piece of linen wrapped around the waist and tied in a decorative knot.

▶ Wealthy Egyptians wore long robes of pleated linen.

MAKE A MAGIC EYE CHARM

You will need:
self-hardening modelling clay
length of leather strip or thick cord
pencil   poster paints
paintbrush   varnish

1. Knead the clay until soft and then shape into the charm.

2. Add extra clay for the pupil of the eye and at the top of the charm. Use the pencil to make the top piece into a loop.

3. Leave the clay to harden. Paint in bright colours and leave to dry.

4. Varnish, then thread the leather strip or cord through the loop and wear your charm for extra luck.

70 **Sandals were made from papyrus and other reeds.** Kings and queens, rich people and courtiers wore padded leather ones. Footwear was a luxury item, and most ordinary people walked around barefoot. Colourful pictures of sandals were even painted onto the feet of mummies!

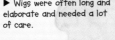

▶ Wigs were often long and elaborate and needed a lot of care.

▼ Egyptians cared for their wigs with combs made of wood and ivory. They used ivory pins to keep their hair in place.

Ivory comb

Ivory hair pins

Wooden comb

71 **Wealthy people wore wigs made from human hair or sheep's wool.** Wigs were kept on a stand when not being worn. Girls wore their hair in pigtails, while boys mostly had shaved heads, sometimes with a plaited lock on one side.

Baking and brewing

72 **Bread was the most important food.** Harvested grain was stored in granaries until needed. Beer was the most popular drink. It was very thick and had to be strained before drinking. Models of brewers were left in tombs to ensure the dead person had plenty of beer in the next world!

▼ Beer was made from grain and water. Egyptian beer did not keep well and needed to be drunk within a day or two.

Workers treading on grain and water mixture

Water and grain fermenting in jars

The fermented brew is sieved to remove pieces of grain

Water is poured into a jar of grain to be mixed

BANQUET MENU

A huge choice of food was served at banquets for wealthy Egyptians. Meats such as duck, goose, gazelle and heron, fresh fruits and vegetables, sweet pastries and cakes, with lots of beer and grape or date wine to drink. Choose the food for a banquet and design a decorative menu for your guests.

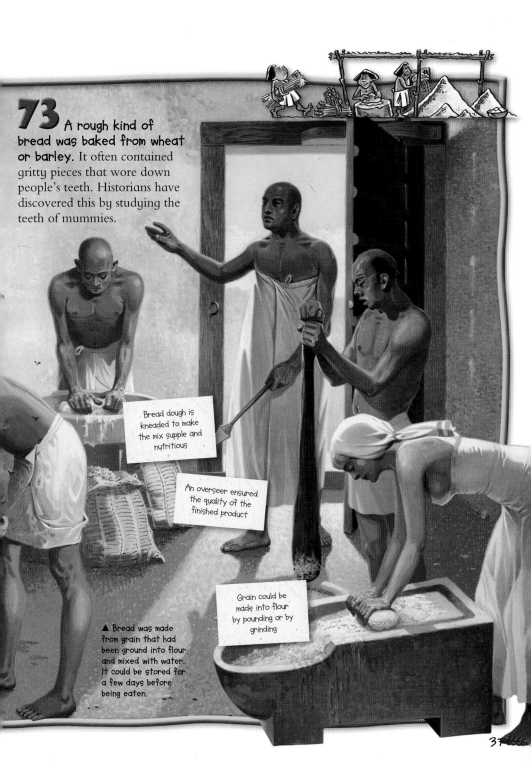

73 **A rough kind of bread was baked from wheat or barley.** It often contained gritty pieces that wore down people's teeth. Historians have discovered this by studying the teeth of mummies.

Bread dough is kneaded to make the mix supple and nutritious

An overseer ensured the quality of the finished product

Grain could be made into flour by pounding or by grinding

▲ Bread was made from grain that had been ground into flour and mixed with water. It could be stored for a few days before being eaten.

Hard day's work

74 Scribes were very important people. These highly skilled men kept records of everything that happened from day to day. They recorded the materials used for building work, the number of cattle, and the crops that had been gathered for the royal family, the government and the temples.

75 Libraries in ancient Egypt held thousands of papyrus scrolls. They covered subjects such as law, astronomy, medicine and geography. Most Egyptians could not read or write, so libraries were used by educated people such as scribes and doctors.

76 Imagine if there were 700 letters in the alphabet! That was how many hieroglyphs Egyptian school children had to learn. Hieroglyphs were symbols that the Egyptians used for writing. Some symbols stood for words and some for sounds. Only boys went to schools for scribes, where they first learned how to read and write hieroglyphs.

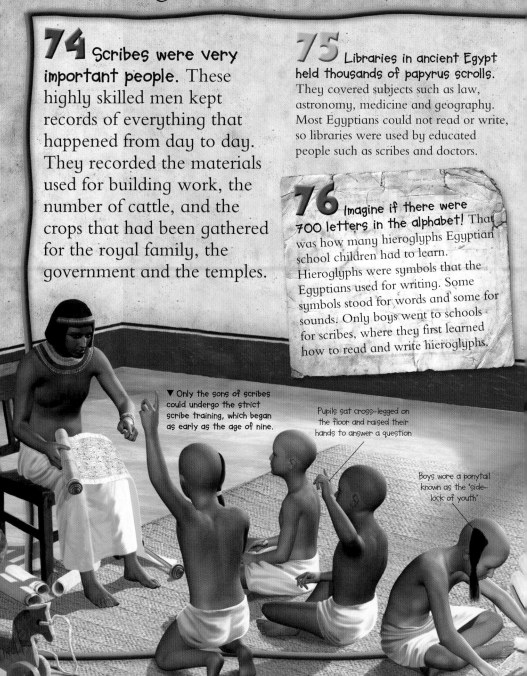

▼ Only the sons of scribes could undergo the strict scribe training, which began as early as the age of nine.

Pupils sat cross-legged on the floor and raised their hands to answer a question

Boys wore a ponytail known as the 'side-lock of youth'

77 **Most people worked as craftworkers or farm labourers.** Craftworkers included carpenters, potters, weavers, jewellers, shoemakers, glassblowers and perfume makers. Many sold their goods from small shops in the towns. They were kept busy making items for the pharaoh and wealthy people.

▶ Craftworkers produced statues and furniture for the pharaoh. Workers such as these often had their own areas within a town. The village of Deir el-Medina was built specially for those who worked on tombs in the Valley of the Kings.

78 **A typical lunch for a worker consisted of bread and onions.** They may also have had a cucumber, washed down with a drink of beer.

80 **Slaves were often prisoners who were captured from enemies.** They also came from the countries of Kush and Nubia. Life as a slave was not all bad. A slave could own land and buy goods – and even buy his freedom.

79 **The base of the Great Pyramid takes up almost as much space as five football pitches!** Huge quantities of stone were needed to build these monuments. The Egyptians quarried limestone, sandstone and granite for their buildings. In the surrounding desert they mined gold for decorations.

Clever Egyptians

81 The insides of many Egyptian tombs were decorated with brightly coloured wall paintings. The scenes showed what the Egyptians hoped life in the next world would be like.

▲ The Egyptians believed that these wall paintings would come to life in the next world.

82 Sculptors carved enormous statues of their pharaohs and gods. Stone statues up to 20 metres tall were placed outside tombs or temples to guard the entrance. Inside a tomb was a small wooden statue of the dead person where the ka, or life force, of the person could rest. Inside temples the holiest statue of a god would be made of silver, ivory or gold.

▲ Huge stone statues guard the entrance to the temple of Abu Simbel. When the temple was rediscovered in 1817, it was almost covered by sand.

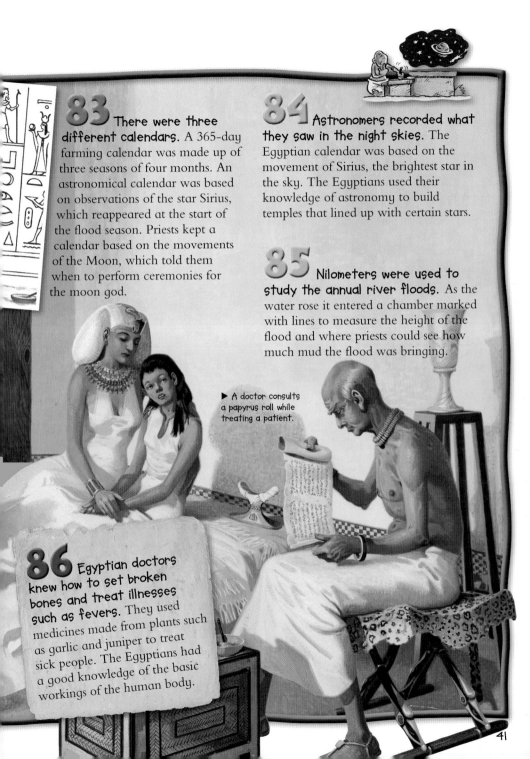

83 There were three different calendars. A 365-day farming calendar was made up of three seasons of four months. An astronomical calendar was based on observations of the star Sirius, which reappeared at the start of the flood season. Priests kept a calendar based on the movements of the Moon, which told them when to perform ceremonies for the moon god.

84 Astronomers recorded what they saw in the night skies. The Egyptian calendar was based on the movement of Sirius, the brightest star in the sky. The Egyptians used their knowledge of astronomy to build temples that lined up with certain stars.

85 Nilometers were used to study the annual river floods. As the water rose it entered a chamber marked with lines to measure the height of the flood and where priests could see how much mud the flood was bringing.

▶ A doctor consults a papyrus roll while treating a patient.

86 Egyptian doctors knew how to set broken bones and treat illnesses such as fevers. They used medicines made from plants such as garlic and juniper to treat sick people. The Egyptians had a good knowledge of the basic workings of the human body.

From pictures to words

87 The Egyptians had no paper – they wrote on papyrus. It was made from papyrus reeds that grew on the banks of the Nile. At first papyrus was sold as long strips, or scrolls, tied with string. Later, papyrus sheets were put into books. Papyrus lasts a long time – sheets have survived 3000 years to the present day.

88 Ink was made by mixing water with soot, charcoal or coloured minerals. Scribes wrote in ink on papyrus scrolls, using reed brushes with specially shaped ends.

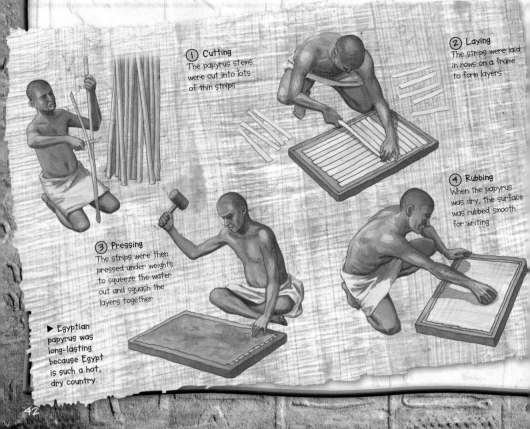

① Cutting
The papyrus stems were cut into lots of thin strips

② Laying
The strips were laid in rows on a frame to form layers

③ Pressing
The strips were then pressed under weights to squeeze the water out and squash the layers together

④ Rubbing
When the papyrus was dry, the surface was rubbed smooth for writing

▶ Egyptian papyrus was long-lasting because Egypt is such a hot, dry country.

89
The Rosetta Stone was found in 1799 by a French soldier in Egypt. It is a large stone onto which three kinds of writing have been carved: hieroglyphics, demotics (a simpler form of hieroglyphics), and Greek. All three sets of writing give an account of the coronation of King Ptolemy V.

▲ The Rosetta Stone in the British Museum. The stone itself is made of granite, and is a broken part of a bigger slab.

90
In the 5th century BC a Greek historian called Herodotus wrote about life in ancient Egypt. As he travelled across the country he observed and wrote about people's daily lives, and their religion and customs such as embalming and mummification.

▼ The name of Rameses II written inside a cartouche to show he was a pharaoh.

91
The hieroglyphs of a ruler's name were written inside an oval-shaped frame called a cartouche. The pharaoh's cartouche was carved on pillars and temple walls, painted on tomb walls and mummy cases, and written on official documents.

92
The Egyptians used a system of picture writing called hieroglyphics. Each hieroglyph represented an object or a sound. For example, the picture of a lion represented the sound 'l' and a basket represented the word 'lord'. Scribes wrote hieroglyphs on papyrus scrolls or carved them into stone.

PICTURE-WRITING
Below is a hieroglyphic alphabet. The name 'Jane' has been written in hieroglyphs. Can you write your name?

Fun and games

93 **Hippo hunting was a dangerous but popular sport.**
Hunters in boats, armed only with spears and ropes, killed hippos in the waters of the Nile. In the desert, hunters chased lions, antelope and wild bulls. Marsh birds were killed with throwing sticks that were like boomerangs.

MAKE A SNAKE GAME

You will need:
sheet of thick cardboard   large dinner plate
paintbrush   scissors   coloured pens
yellow paint   counters   pencil   two dice

Place the plate on the card and draw round the outside. Ask an adult to help cut out the circle. Paint one side with paint. Leave to dry.

Draw a snake's head in the centre of the circle. Draw small circles spreading out from the centre until you reach the edge of the cardboard. Colour the circles in.

Give each player a counter. Throw the dice and take turns to move along the circles. The winner is the first one to reach the snake's head.

▼ Hunting was reserved mostly for royalty and courtiers. Amenhotep III was said to have killed more than 100 lions in ten years.

94 **The Egyptians played a board game called senet.** The game represented the struggle between good and evil on the journey into the next world. Players moved sets of counters across the board according to how their throwing sticks (like modern dice) landed.

▶ A senet game found in an Egyptian tomb.

Heroes and heroines

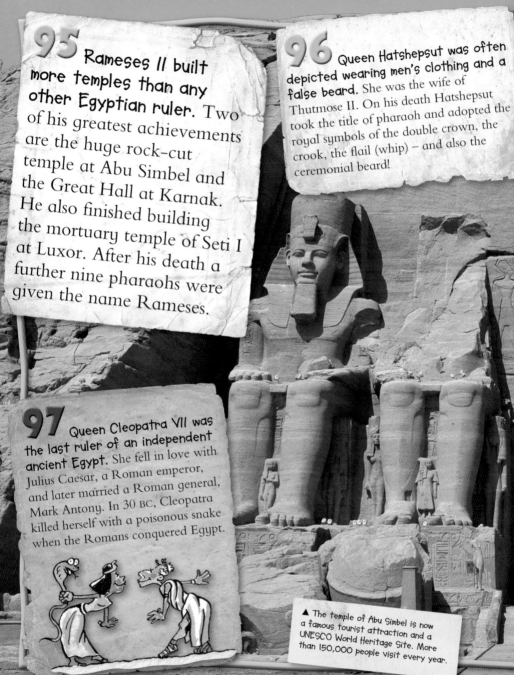

95 **Rameses II built more temples than any other Egyptian ruler.** Two of his greatest achievements are the huge rock-cut temple at Abu Simbel and the Great Hall at Karnak. He also finished building the mortuary temple of Seti I at Luxor. After his death a further nine pharaohs were given the name Rameses.

96 **Queen Hatshepsut was often depicted wearing men's clothing and a false beard.** She was the wife of Thutmose II. On his death Hatshepsut took the title of pharaoh and adopted the royal symbols of the double crown, the crook, the flail (whip) – and also the ceremonial beard!

97 **Queen Cleopatra VII was the last ruler of an independent ancient Egypt.** She fell in love with Julius Caesar, a Roman emperor, and later married a Roman general, Mark Antony. In 30 BC, Cleopatra killed herself with a poisonous snake when the Romans conquered Egypt.

▲ The temple of Abu Simbel is now a famous tourist attraction and a UNESCO World Heritage Site. More than 150,000 people visit every year.

98 Tutankhamun is probably the most famous pharaoh of all. His tomb, with its fabulous treasure of over 5000 objects, was discovered complete in 1922. Tutankhamun was only nine years old when he became ruler, and he died at the young age of about 17. He was buried in the Valley of the Kings.

▶ The head of of Tutankhamun's mummy was covered by a mask made of solid gold, and decorated with jewels.

99 King Menes was the first ruler of a united Egypt. He joined together the kingdoms of Upper and Lower Egypt, under one government, in around 3100 BC. Menes was also called Narmer. Archaeologists have found a slate tablet, called the Narmer Palette, that shows him beating his enemies in battle.

100 Thutmose III was a clever general who added new lands to ancient Egypt. Under his leadership, Egypt's armies seized territory in Syria to the north and Palestine to the east. During his reign Thutmose ordered a giant obelisk made of granite to be placed at Heliopolis – it now stands on the bank of the river Thames in London.

Index